Out and About Activity Book

KINGFISHER

Castles

By
Gillian Osband
Illustrations by
Dave Simonds

Contents

KINGFISHER BOOKS

Looking at Castles

Before 1066, when William of Normandy conquered England, there were few castles in Britain. But by 1086, 90 stone castles and many more wooden ones had been built all over the country. And that was just the start!

William's castles were meant to stop the native Saxons rebelling. They were often built close to Saxon towns and on high ground to give a good view over the surrounding area. When you next visit a castle see if you can discover if there were any special reasons for its position.

Some castles, like the one at Shrewsbury, were built in towns to provide a local centre for defence and administration in the area.

Castle Acre in Norfolk was set in open country to avoid a surprise attack. It was built as the headquarters for a Norman baron.

Some castles were built to guard harbours – Abereinon Castle, in Dyfed, is one. Camber Castle, Sussex is another, but here the sea receded a long time ago and it is now surrounded by fields!

The ruined Norman castle at Richmond in Yorkshire was built on a hill. From this position it could guard the valley of the River Swale.

Where possible, a castle would make good use of any natural defences. Cilgerran Castle, in Dyfed, was built at the top of a gorge.

Bodiam Castle, in Sussex, was built near a river so it could have a wide moat. But it never actually had to defend itself against attack.

In Cambridgeshire, Alrehede Castle, near the Aldreth Causeway was built above a narrow pass to defend it from attack.

Caernarfon Castle in Gwynedd was built by King Edward I in the 13th century, to mark the defeat of the Welsh princes and to bring

North Wales under English control. Wales has many of these fortress castles, most were built along the English border to stop rebellions.

Different Kinds of Castles

Even after William was crowned king, he did not have control of the whole country – the Saxons regarded him as the enemy. So he rewarded his followers with land he had taken from Saxon earls, in return for which they promised to obey him and to provide knights to fight for him. This meant his people were in positions of power, but they had to build their castles quickly so that any Saxon rebellions could be crushed.

Motte and Bailey

These were the first castles built after the conquest. They were cheap and quick to build, with the conquered Saxons to do the work.
1. First deep V-shaped ditches would be dug, and the earth thrown inwards to make a mound – the motte. Most mottes were about 5 metres high.

2. A wooden tower – the keep – was built on top of the motte. It was sometimes just for defence, but also usually contained the lord's living quarters and the stores. The keep was often painted or plastered to look like stone. A wooden fence was built around the keep, but later stone was used.

3. Other domestic buildings were in the bailey, a fenced-off area at the foot of the motte that often had a ditch around it too. The main kitchens were in the bailey because of the risk of fire. A bridge or gate between the motte and the bailey allowed the motte to be sealed off for extra defence.

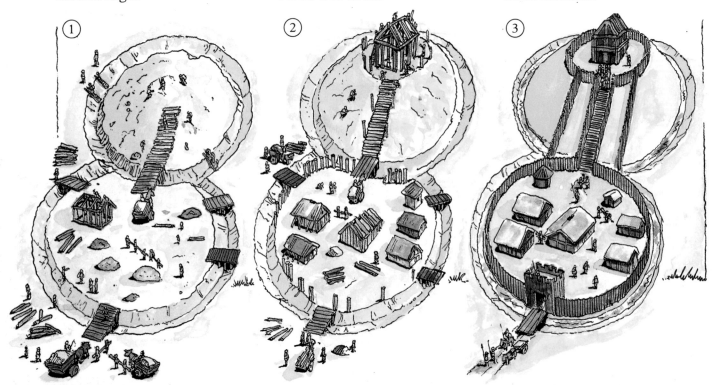

Curtain wall

Turret

Portcullis

Gatehouse

Arrow loops

Square Stone Keeps

These replaced the wooden keeps and were bigger – up to 35 metres high, with three or four storeys and spiral staircases in the corner turrets.

The way into the keep was through the forebuilding, which contained stairs to the first floor. The Great Hall, the Lord's bedroom and solar (study) and the chapel were placed here. The soldiers lived on the top floor and the ground floor was for stores, and prisoners.

The windows were thin slits, but arrows could be fired out through them. Around the keep was a strong wall, called a curtain wall, with a gatehouse. Inside the gate was a thick metal grille called a portcullis.

Forebuilding

Plinth – to prevent battering rams from reaching the walls

Battering ram – for breaking down walls or gates

Building a Castle

Many workers were needed to build a castle, including masons, smiths, carpenters and well-diggers. It was vital for the castle to have a well in case of attack.

The walls were made of two layers of stone filled with rubble and mortar in between. In Dover Castle, in Kent, the walls are about 6 metres thick!

Once the walls were finished they were coated with plaster or painted. Everything had to be done by hand and the tools were very simple. Pulleys and wooden scaffolding were used to make things easier.

The Final Solution

Over the next 200 years castles gradually changed. The improvements were partly due to ideas brought back by knights who had fought in the Crusades – a series of campaigns to capture Palestine from the Turks. When Edward I returned to England, he brought back the perfect design – known as the concentric castle. Caerphilly Castle, in Wales is a fine example.

Concentric Castles

Concentric castles were built around an open area in the centre, and not around a keep, as Norman castles were.

The centre was called the inner bailey and was protected by a wall. Inside was a well, the Great Hall and other buildings.

Around the inner wall was an empty area of land called the outer bailey. Then came the second, outer wall with a drawbridge and barbican.

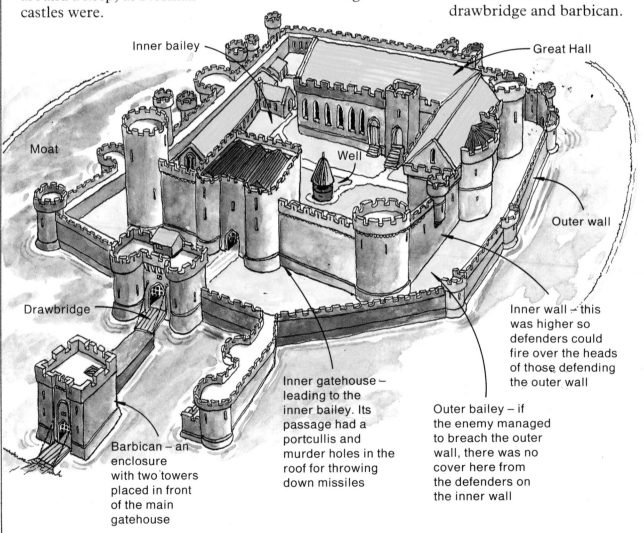

Inner bailey

Great Hall

Moat

Well

Outer wall

Drawbridge

Inner wall – this was higher so defenders could fire over the heads of those defending the outer wall

Barbican – an enclosure with two towers placed in front of the main gatehouse

Inner gatehouse – leading to the inner bailey. Its passage had a portcullis and murder holes in the roof for throwing down missiles

Outer bailey – if the enemy managed to breach the outer wall, there was no cover here from the defenders on the inner wall

Castle Clues

When you visit a castle try to find clues that will help you to imagine what it was really like when people lived and worked there, and depended on it for their protection. Here are some things to look out for.

Merlon

Crenel

Arrow loop

Swinging shutter

The Curtain Wall

This was the main defence of the castle. The sentry walk, where the soldiers kept watch, would have been at least 2 metres thick. There were gaps in the battlements, called crenels, so the soldiers could see the enemy and take cover behind the higher merlons. Arrow loops were for shooting through, and swinging wooden shutters could be hung across the crenels to give extra cover.

If there was a moat, look for holes above the entrance arch where the chains to raise and lower the drawbridge were. This would be an important part of the castle's defences.

Inside the Keep

If the castle has a keep, look for the things shown above. There should be fireplaces (1) on each floor. Beam holes (2) show where the joists under the floor were. You may see a spiral staircase (3) in a turret wall (4). Inside a turret, look for rooms used as stores, bedrooms, garderobes (toilets) or kitchens.

The chapel was often inside the keep. Look for a stone basin set in a wall, stone seats or decorative arches along the side of a wall.

The Gatehouse

This was the best defended place in the castle. Look for grooves where a portcullis fitted, or machicolations – overhanging galleries with holes for dropping things on enemies.

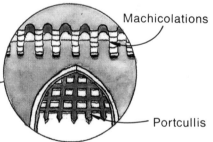

Machicolations

Portcullis

The Inner Bailey

In a castle without a keep, look for the Great Hall – it will have large windows and fireplaces against the inner curtain wall. In the kitchens, look for a fireplace large enough to roast a whole ox, perhaps with a small bread oven at the back. You may even find a sink set into the wall and some drains.

Make a Castle Plan

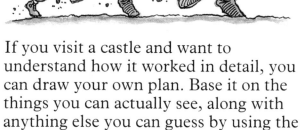

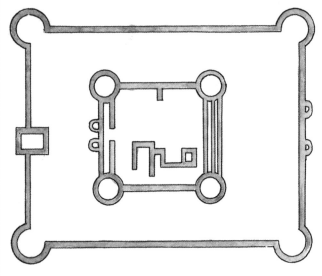

 Well

 Chapel

 Dungeon

 Portcullis

 Drawbridge

 Lord's chamber

If you visit a castle and want to understand how it worked in detail, you can draw your own plan. Base it on the things you can actually see, along with anything else you can guess by using the clues explained on page 7.

First of all walk around the walls and draw an outline of their shape. Do you think the castle is one of the types described in this book, or is it a mixture of styles, with bits added on at later stages? You can sometimes see that this has happened where a different colour of stone has been used.

Once you have drawn a floor plan, try and work out where the important rooms would have been, and draw them in on your plan, using symbols like the ones shown here.

Design Your Own Castle

If you have looked at a few castles, you can probably work out what the weak points might have been. Imagine you are a 13th-century lord – can you design the perfect castle to provide safety from attack and a comfortable home? Remember – the position you choose is as important as the design of the castle itself.

Castle Quiz

1. **W** _ _ _ _ _ **R**
Castle, England

2. **C** _ _ _ _ _ _ _ _ **N**
Castle, Wales

3. **C** _ _ _ **E**
Castle, England

Can you try and guess the missing letters from the names of these famous castles? Look carefully at the drawings, they will give you a clue, too.

Answers on page 24.

4. **P** _ _ _ _ _ _ **E**
Castle, Wales

5. **B** _ _ _ _ _ _ **L**
Castle, Scotland

Hidden Words

There are 12 words to do with castles hidden in the square. Try and find them using the clues below.

Answers on page 24.

1. Best protected part (9)
2. Place to .... you safe (4)
3. Could be inner or outer (6)
4. A mound of earth (5)
5. A knight carries one (6)
6. Down for friend, up for foe (10)
7. Don't fall in! (4)
8. At the corner of 2 (6)
9. Made gates strong (10)
10. Another name for a study (5)
11. Everyone visits this room at some time (9)
12. The outer wall had one (8)

```
G D C B P H H M D L Q G F M F A M A H N E G O O C L
N O L C M G A O F K P M F M G C G H K B I M D M B L
F M Q I M Q Q A N B N C M N J I E M P H B O T H M N
A K A Q S H E T H H K D H M N F O B E D O M U F H O
L E Q F E H G A T E H O U S E N E J I D D G R Q J L
P N A N H K K H N J Q D J B B A G H L L Q B R L J C
N P I D I P Q M K G C N E P H H H I E B G M E D M G
Q Q Q N H P A I N E F Q N K A G P I B Q N O T J B C
C D O N N Q B Q M N J E P L K Q P P F B L B P N O K
B D G S O C Q M F K K K E E P L O I G L H Q B J H N
F C H O C K P F B B E C P G H K R L A O L M E E A F
M C Q L E E N L G H N C H D F B T P M M E Q P L B O
M M Q A B L C J I K I M L E A A C O K D G E Q P Q O
B D L R E O C B B B A I L E Y K U Q H F A K L F Q K
Q D A B Q A B Q M B D H B G H A L G N O R H Q C H K
A K B M B E O P D M P G H H A B L E G N D G C O D L
F I A D G H I D B C L P H F D N I Q N K E P F M Q H
C N R M N L J G D L N M O T T E S P O F R L N Q E E
Q J B K H D O I P E I N N O I G H H F N O I G E B A
F Q I P Q I C C E Q S H I E L D P B E E B N B H F E
F G C Q K D C E B O O S H G K N O Q P I E H D J L P
D O A D K P P J N O J Q Q E D C M L O I H K E O L F
J Q N H M B N E A P J M A Q F Q B P O J K C G E E E
D E O L A G L L M H I A D R A W B R I D G E M K K G
H K I O L G E K Q M E E D L M K N G K I F H H C A F
```

9

Who Lived in a Castle?

Building and running castles was a very expensive business. Eventually only the king could afford to build new castles, and the nobles just carried on with the ones they already had. A minor lord probably had just one where he lived all year, but a lord with several castles would spend a few months in each before moving on with his family and servants.

The Lord and family

5 Male Servants

5 Female Servants

10 Knights

3 Huntsmen

Treasurer

Chaplain

3 Falconers

6 Esquires

4 Grooms

4 Cooks

When the lord and his family moved castle, they took with them all the servants shown here – there might be 50 people in all. On top of this, each castle had a permanent staff to keep it running when the lord was not there. There would be a steward, who acted as the lord's deputy, a chaplain, domestic servants, a smith, a mason and a carpenter, a groom, an armourer, all with their apprentices, and sometimes a small garrison of soldiers.

Feeding a Castle

In a well-run castle the steward prepared for his lord's stay by making sure the stores were full of food. When the stores became low and the hunting was finished, or the castle started to smell (plumbing was not too good in those days), the Lord and his household just moved on to the next castle.

The food they ate came from the lord's land, where his peasants would usually work two days a week for him as payment for the land they rented.

The lord lived quite well. Sheep, pigs and cows were kept for meat, cows and goats for milk. Only the lord and his family could hunt – deer, boar and hares. Oats, barley or wheat were grown, also apples, plums, pears and vegetables such as parsnips. Bees gave honey, and spices and salt were bought from traders.

The arms of
Richard I

Coats of Arms

It was vital for a knight dressed in armour to be recognized by his men, especially in a battle. The men had to know at a glance who to follow and who to attack.

The Company
of Plumbers

The City of
Oxford

Knights wore special badges and carried banners with their own colours and symbols on them, called shields of arms. They also wore sleeveless coats over their armour, bearing the same pattern or picture. These were the first coats of arms.

Heraldry is the name given to the study of these symbols and patterns, and the rules governing their use.

Charge — In chief — Sinister side — Dexter side — Field — In base

Shields and Their Symbols

The shield is the shape which carries the design. The main parts of the shield are shown above right. The design is called the charge. The simplest are known as ordinaries (right).

If a wife had arms of her own, they might be combined with her husband's to make a new shield. Sometimes the charge was an animal, such as a lion (usually used by a king), a gryphon or dragon.

The colours have special names – red is called 'gules', blue is 'azure', silver is 'argent' and gold is 'or'.

Only the king could grant the right to carry a coat of arms. Sometimes loyal merchants or craftsmen were given this right. Their charge might show you what they did, for example a barrel for a wine merchant.

A fesse   A bend   A saltaire   Per fesse   Per bend

Lord's arms + Lady's arms = Combined arms   A gryphon   A dragon

The artist's coat of arms, made up for this book.

Your Own Coat of Arms

Design a coat of arms for your family. If your father is a builder show his tools in the charge. If your mother is a baker you could make combined arms with a cake and trowel! Or make one for yourself with your interests and favourite colours. See if other people recognize it as yours.

How They Lived

During the 12th and 13th centuries, castle defences were improved and they became safer places to live. But they were still pretty uncomfortable, cold and smelly. Life in a castle was very different to life nowadays.

How Did They Cook?

The kitchen was large, as many people had to be fed. It had two or three fireplaces – one big enough to roast an ox. Bread would be baked in an oven at the back. Meat was roasted on a spit; stews and vegetables were cooked in bronze pots. Lots of spices were used, particularly in winter, when the taste of bad meat had to be disguised.

Kitchen and servants carrying food to the Great Hall.

In the Great Hall

This was the centre of castle life, where feasts took place, the lord held court and gave his judgements, and took care of his estates.

Feasts began at about 5.00pm. There might be six meat courses with 20 dishes for each course. The food was often served on slabs of bread, called trenchers.

Pages served food, starting at the high table. People ate messily and threw unwanted food and bones on the floor. Bundles of rushes soaked in fat were burned to give light.

12

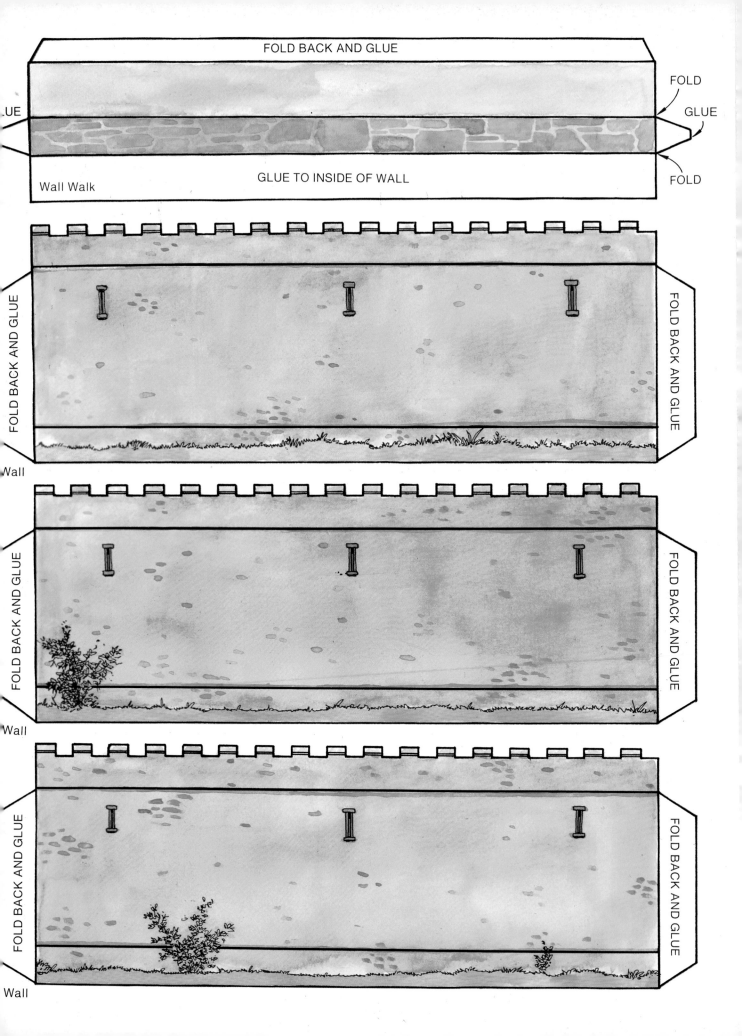

FOLD BACK AND GLUE

FOLD

GLUE

GLUE

FOLD

Wall Walk

GLUE TO INSIDE OF WALL

FOLD BACK AND GLUE

FOLD BACK AND GLUE

Wall

FOLD BACK AND GLUE

FOLD BACK AND GLUE

Wall

FOLD BACK AND GLUE

FOLD BACK AND GLUE

Wall

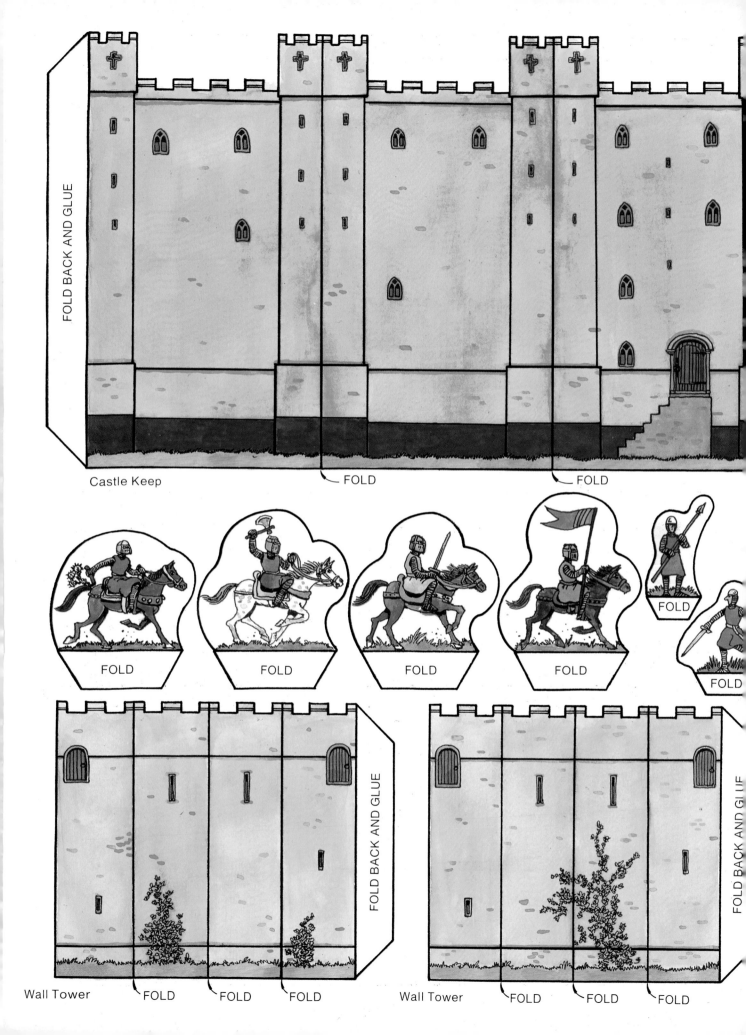

FOLD BACK AND GLUE

Castle Keep   FOLD   FOLD

FOLD   FOLD   FOLD   FOLD   FOLD

FOLD BACK AND GLUE   FOLD BACK AND GLUE

Wall Tower   FOLD   FOLD   FOLD   Wall Tower   FOLD   FOLD   FOLD

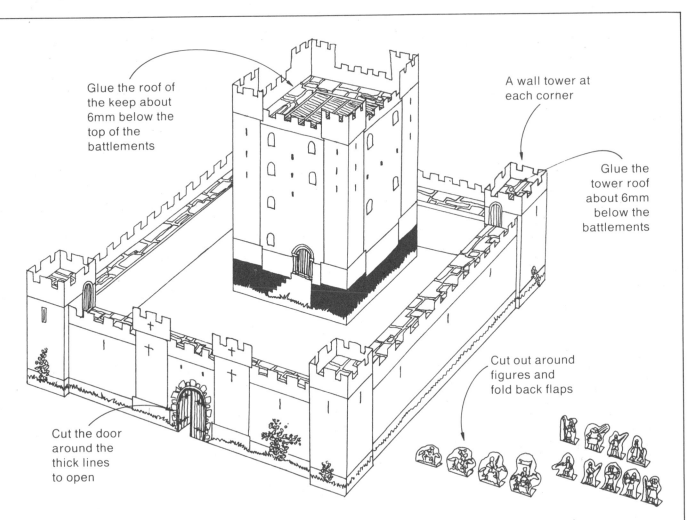

Glue the roof of
the keep about
6mm below the
top of the
battlements

A wall tower at
each corner

Glue the
tower roof
about 6mm
below the
battlements

Cut out around
figures and
fold back flaps

Cut the door
around the
thick lines
to open

4. Glue one of the wall walks to each wall. Then glue the walls and towers together to make a square.

5. Cut carefully around each figure and fold the bottom flaps back, so they stand up. Paint the backs if you wish.

6. Stand your finished castle on a sheet of card, on which you can paint muddy or grassy ground, or a moat.

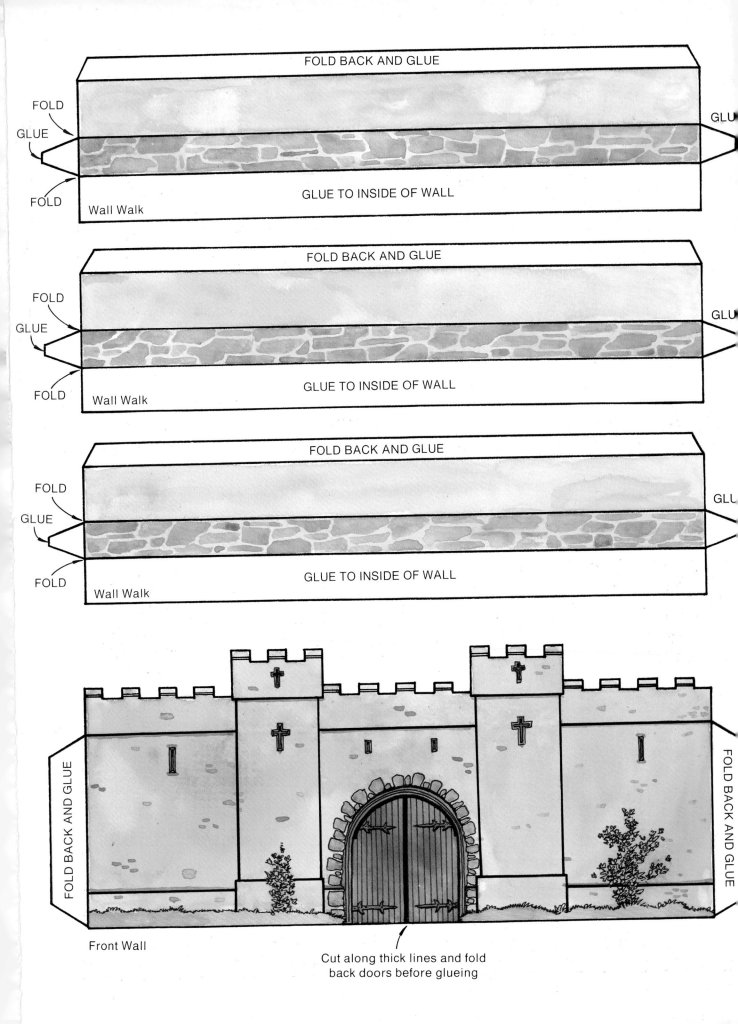

FOLD BACK AND GLUE

FOLD

GLUE

GLU

FOLD

Wall Walk

GLUE TO INSIDE OF WALL

FOLD BACK AND GLUE

FOLD

GLUE

GLU

FOLD

Wall Walk

GLUE TO INSIDE OF WALL

FOLD BACK AND GLUE

FOLD

GLUE

GLU

FOLD

Wall Walk

GLUE TO INSIDE OF WALL

FOLD BACK AND GLUE

FOLD BACK AND GLUE

Front Wall

Cut along thick lines and fold
back doors before glueing

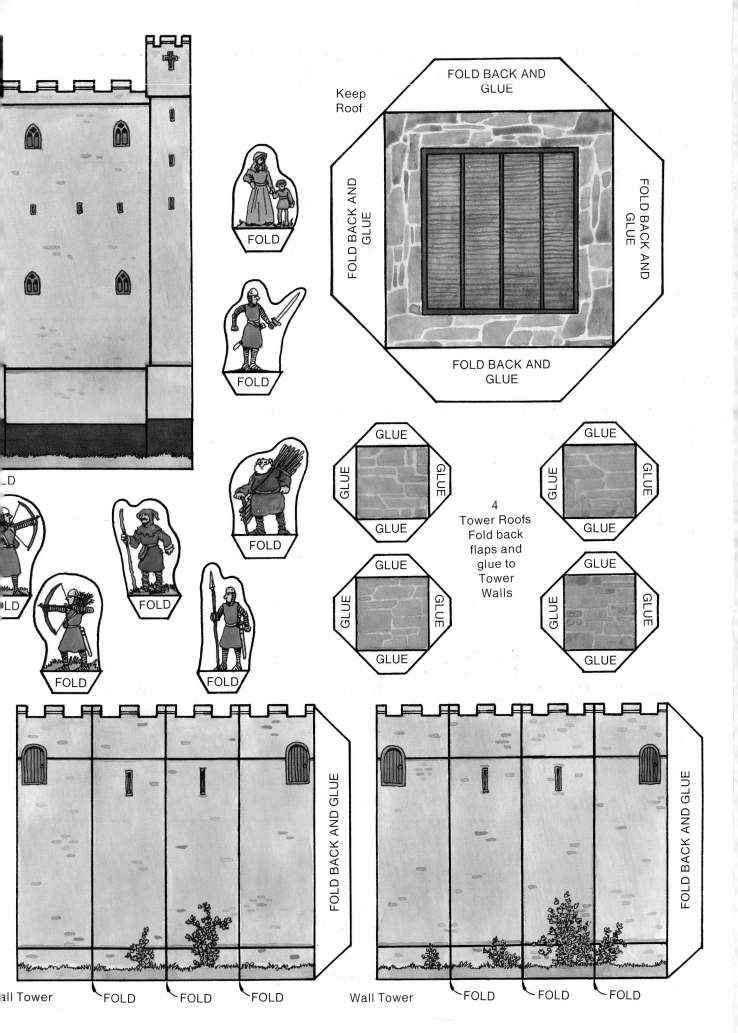

Keep Roof

FOLD BACK AND GLUE

FOLD BACK AND GLUE

FOLD BACK AND GLUE

FOLD BACK AND GLUE

FOLD

FOLD

FOLD

FOLD

FOLD

FOLD

FOLD

FOLD

GLUE
GLUE
GLUE
GLUE

GLUE
GLUE
GLUE
GLUE

4 Tower Roofs Fold back flaps and glue to Tower Walls

GLUE
GLUE
GLUE
GLUE

GLUE
GLUE
GLUE
GLUE

FOLD BACK AND GLUE

FOLD BACK AND GLUE

Wall Tower

Wall Tower

FOLD   FOLD   FOLD

FOLD   FOLD   FOLD

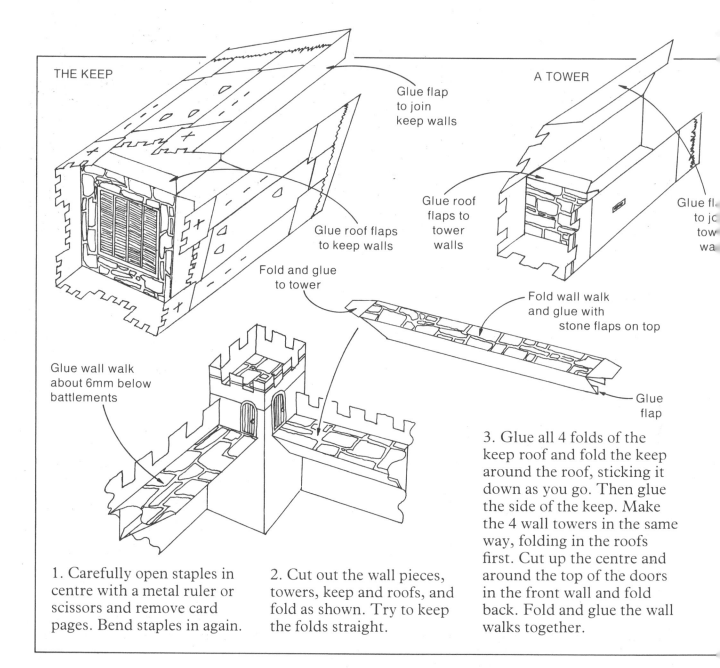

THE KEEP

Glue flap to join keep walls

A TOWER

Glue roof flaps to keep walls

Glue roof flaps to tower walls

Glue fl. to jc tow wa

Fold and glue to tower

Fold wall walk and glue with stone flaps on top

Glue wall walk about 6mm below battlements

Glue flap

1. Carefully open staples in centre with a metal ruler or scissors and remove card pages. Bend staples in again.

2. Cut out the wall pieces, towers, keep and roofs, and fold as shown. Try to keep the folds straight.

3. Glue all 4 folds of the keep roof and fold the keep around the roof, sticking it down as you go. Then glue the side of the keep. Make the 4 wall towers in the same way, folding in the roofs first. Cut up the centre and around the top of the doors in the front wall and fold back. Fold and glue the wall walks together.

How Did They Wash?

For a bath they used a large wooden chest or a barrel filled with water heated on a fire and poured in using buckets. They used soap made of lard and wood ash.

Ladies bathed quite often, with the lord's wife using the water first, and then the other women taking their turn. Until the 13th century, most fighting men did not bath at all because they thought it reduced their strength.

King John had his own travelling bath and bathman, and bathed 11 times a year!

The lord and his family may have had their own garderobe (toilet) by their bedroom. But a big garrison might have used a whole garderobe tower.

The garderobe had a stone or wooden seat with a hole in it over a long chute, or, if it stuck out from the castle wall, over thin air. In summer the garderobe was very smelly.

A Castle Recipe

You need: 175g dried figs, ½ teaspoon powdered cloves, ½ teaspoon ground black pepper, pinch of saffron, 1 dessertspoon honey, 225g pack of shortcrust pastry, flour, bowl, rolling pin, greased baking tray.

1. Cut the figs up and mix with cloves, pepper, honey and saffron in the bowl.
2. Roll out the pastry and cut out rounds. Put some fig mixture on each round.
3. Dampen the edges of the rounds with water. Fold and press the edges together.
4. Preheat your oven to 200° or Gas Mark 6 and bake your tartlets for 20 minutes, or until the pastry is golden brown.
5. Heat four tablespoons of honey with four of water to make a syrup and pour over the tartlets.

Shopping

Castles were quite self-sufficient. Food was grown or caught on the land. Basic tools were made or repaired in the workshops, and women spun and wove material to make clothes. Visiting pedlars brought anything else that was needed such as silk from abroad, spices, jewellery, and news of the outside world.

My Day

It is summer, in the Year of Our Lord 1295. I am Leofric, aged 11, page to Lord William Mountjoy. Here is a record of my day.

Woke up. My turn to fetch the water from the well. A quick wash of my face and hands will do. You won't catch me washing all over, although my lord has started to. Next a quick visit to the garderobe. What a smell, and we're here another month!

6.00am

POO!

7.00am

Had a good breakfast – salted fish, bread and a cup of beer mixed with water.

7.30am

Watched my lord set out for the hunt with his huntsmen, falconers and the guests.

9.00am

Visited the falcons. I hope I'll be allowed to train one if I can get it to trust me.

10.00am

Boring! Two hours of lessons. I can't see why a knight would need to read or write.

12.00am

Lunch. Cook used a lot of spices – but the left-overs had gone off in the heat!

1.00pm

Nearly 60 pieces of armour to clean! Rubbing it with sand and vinegar is smelly work.

I'll start wearing armour from next year, so I can get used to the weight gradually.

3.00pm

Sword practice. I tried my best, but I could hardly lift my sword after that rubbing.

Time off. If Godfrey can beat me at stone skimming, I do his chores tonight. I beat him . . .

4.00pm

Nearly dropped the venison on my lord's guest. My lady isn't pleased – my lord dripped candlewax on her new gown.

5.00pm

There was plenty of food left tonight because of the hunt, even though it was cold. Fell asleep during supper.

8.00pm

Tomorrow Brother Cedric is going to teach us how to write ballads about knightly deeds, and we're going fishing.

8.30pm

Your Day

Make a diary of your day, like Leofric's. Would you rather be a page in a castle?

Think how different your day is from Leofric's. Where did the water come from when you washed? Did you have to clean swords during the day?

Imagine what it would be like if Leofric served your breakfast. What would he think of the way we live now, and how would you explain it to him? Difficult isn't it?

15

Fun and Games

What sports do you play? Football, tennis or hockey?
Do you go skating when your local pond has frozen over?
If you had lived in the 12th century you would have
played the same games – although in a slightly different
version.

Try playing tennis as it was originally – with your hands

Hockey

The old English name was 'bandy ball'. It was a very rough game with no rules at all. To get the ball you hit your opponent with your stick. Richard II banned it in 1388 because it interfered with war training.

Tennis

Tennis was brought to Europe by the Crusaders in the 12th century. The ball was hit directly using the palm of the hand – 'rahat' in Arabic, and the word racquet originates from that.

Before starting to play, you shouted the French word 'tenez', meaning hold, to make sure your opponent was ready, and that gave us the name 'tennis'. A servant would deliver the first ball. Tennis was banned in 1389 and archery encouraged instead.

Dice Games

Games with dice were very popular and people would use them in gambling games to try and win money. Here is an easy game, called Fifty.

You need: two players and two dice.
Each player takes it in turn to roll both dice together, but you only score when the same numbers are thrown – two 1s, two 2s, and so on.

All these doubles, except 3s and 6s score five points. A double 6 scores 25, a double 3 wipes out the player's total and he has to start again. The first to reach 50 wins.

Skating

Skating needed a lot of practice, because the skates were made of iron and often slipped off. Or else they were strapped on so tightly, they cut off the blood to the feet.

16

Chess

As a war game, chess was very popular among both the nobles and the clergy. It originally came from India, but in Europe the pieces were changed to represent the different levels of society in the Middle Ages.

Jolly Jesters

Many kings and lords had full-time jesters to amuse them. These so-called 'fools' sang songs and told jokes, and often passed on gossip no-one else would dare to tell to the king or lord.

Here are some jester jokes:

Why does a wise king have several court jesters?
So he can be sure of having his wits about him.

What did the King say when his enemy fired at him?
That was an arrow escape.

Why is the heir to the throne like a cloudy day?
Because both are certain to rain (reign).

There were also travelling musicians and mummers (actors) who told stories of heroic deeds.

Simple Samplers

All girls could sew. It was considered both a pleasant and a useful activity. They practised sewing by making samplers. Sometimes they arranged the stitches in patterns, but often they made pictures.

You can make a castle sampler of the picture opposite, using simple stitches, such as back stitch, running stitch, cross stitch and satin stitch. Or make up one of your own showing things familiar to you. Sew your name and the date on it. You never know, in a hundred years someone could find it and wonder about your life too.

Armour

It seems as though in the Middle Ages, there was always a fight going on somewhere. But although castles were built to provide the best possible defence, a lot of fighting was done at close quarters so armour was vital for protection.

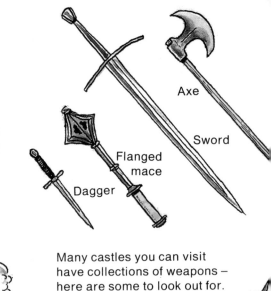

Axe

Sword

Flanged mace

Dagger

Chain mail to protect neck

Helmet

Breastplate

Gauntlet

Armour Facts

Heat and lack of air in a suit of armour could cause problems. Some knights died of heat stroke during battles.

Knights were not lifted onto their horses with a crane. They were used to the weight of armour because they wore it from an early age, when they were still pages. Even so, if a knight fell face down off his horse during battle it would be very difficult for him to get up again.

Leg harness

Many castles you can visit have collections of weapons – here are some to look out for.

Mace

Lance

Pike

Brass Rubbing

Some old churches have pictures of knights made in brass, set into the floors. If you find one, ask permission to make a rubbing – there may be a small charge to pay. You can buy special paper and crayons in art shops.

Use masking tape – not ordinary sticky tape – to hold the paper in place over the brass, then rub gently with a crayon. You should get a clear picture of the knight. Black paper and a white or gold coloured crayon gives a good effect.

Make Your Own

Ears

Nose

Plastic bowl
with foil

Flaps attached
to bowl

Handle

Paint handle
gold

Paint blade
silver

You need: silver foil, sticky
tape, card or cardboard, glue,
paints, a plastic bowl, pencil,
scissors.

Helmet

Make sure the bowl fits easily
on top of your head before
you start. Cover it with silver
foil and tape it in place
inside. Draw ear and nose
pieces on the card and cut
them out. Cover them with
foil too, then tape them in
position on the helmet.

Shield

Draw a shield shape on the
card and cut it out. Decide
what design or charge you
want and paint it on – if you
designed a coat of arms for
yourself, use that.

　　When the paint is dry, turn
the shield over. Cut a strip of
card, long enough to make a
handle for you to hold. Tape
it firmly to the back of the
shield just above the middle.

Sword

Draw a sword shape on stiff
card, and cut it out. Paint the
handle (the proper name is
the hilt) gold or yellow, and
the blade silver or grey. You
can decorate the hilt by
sticking coloured paper on it.

The Whole Thing

A real suit of
armour might have
as many as 60
pieces, but you
can make your
own much more
simply

Bend pieces of
card together to
form tubes. Cover
them with silver
foil or paint them
and tape them on
over your arms
and legs to protect
them

If you have a pair
of old wellingtons
spray them silver
too.

Make a breast-
plate from two
pieces of card.
Punch holes in the
card and tie the
two pieces
together with
string over your
shoulders and
under your arms –
not too tightly.
Paint your charge
on the front and
back.

Use silver spray
paint to make a
pair of old rubber
gloves look like
metal. This can
make a mess so
ask an adult to
help.

Trebuchet

Tunnelling
to weaken
foundations

Mantlet

Siege
tower

Battering
ram

Mangonel

Under Siege

Castles were designed to be strong and easy to defend against attack. But as castles became stronger, so did the weapons used to break down their defences. Brute force was not the only method of defeating a castle though. By mounting a siege, attackers could starve castle dwellers into surrender, so it was important for both sides to be well prepared.

Getting Ready to Attack

Attempting to take a castle defended by a strong garrison could be a very expensive and complicated affair.

Miners might be needed for tunnelling under the castle walls. Timber would have to be felled to make the special assault weapons needed for the attack. Stone would be needed for missiles to be hurled into the castle using siege machines.

Lastly the besieging force would need food, water and shelter for them and their horses for as long as the siege continued.

Getting Ready to Defend

Inside the castle the most important thing was to have enough food. Salted meat, fish and grain were stored in bulk, along with beer and wine.

Before the attack began cows, goats and sheep would be driven into the inner bailey to give milk, cheese and meat.

Having clean water was also vital, so the wells would have to be protected. Nonetheless, disease was often a problem.

Make a Siege Catapult

You will need:
an empty milk carton,
a pair of scissors,
two pencils,
a small elastic band,
a safety match,
an empty matchbox,
sticky tape.

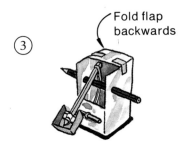

Small hole

1. Carefully cut the top off the milk carton, leaving a flap at the front and cutting the back down lower, as shown. Make a hole in both sides for a pencil to go through and a smaller hole in the back.

2. Push pencil 1 through the holes in the sides, thread the elastic band through the small hole and hold it in place with the match. Cut the inside drawer of the matchbox in half and tape pencil 2 inside it.

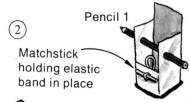

Pencil 1

Matchstick holding elastic band in place

Pencil 2

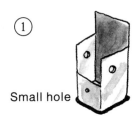

Fold flap backwards

3. Loop the elastic band over the bottom of pencil 2, with pencil 2 in front of pencil 1, so that when you pull the top of pencil 2 back it pivots on pencil 1 and the elastic band is stretched tightly. Now tape the front flap down.

4. Pull pencil 2 right back, put a piece of screwed up silver foil or paper in the matchbox and let go. Now all you need is a castle to attack!

Taken Prisoner

Few castles had specially built prisons. Most used part of the store rooms, which could only be entered from above and were dark and cold. If there were any proper prisons they would be in the gatehouse, where plenty of guards were always on duty. Prisoners being held hostage for ransom or favours had to be well looked after. But for prisoners who had committed crimes, conditions were terrible.

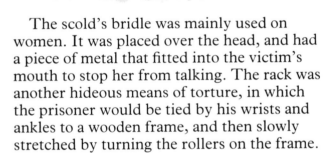

Thumbscrews

Scold's bridle

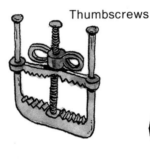

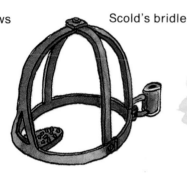

Torture

Torture was never lawful in England, but sometimes the ruler and lords put themselves above the law, and used horrible means to punish people or make them confess to crimes they may or may not have committed!

Thumbscrews were used, as you can probably guess, to squash people's thumbs.

The scold's bridle was mainly used on women. It was placed over the head, and had a piece of metal that fitted into the victim's mouth to stop her from talking. The rack was another hideous means of torture, in which the prisoner would be tied by his wrists and ankles to a wooden frame, and then slowly stretched by turning the rollers on the frame.

The rack

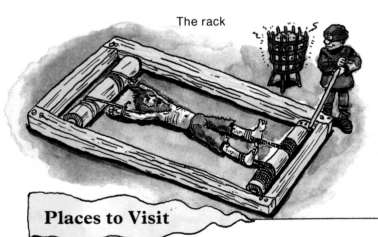

Places to Visit

You can visit dungeons, prisons and torture chambers in lots of castles, try: The Tower of London; Hever Castle, Kent; Warwick Castle, Warwick; Bolton Castle, North Yorkshire; Corfe Castle, Dorset; Braemar Castle, Grampian; Alnwick Castle, Northumberland.

Prison Graffitti

When you visit a prison or dungeon look out for initials, dates or sometimes pictures carved on the walls. On a wall in the Tower of London, more than 100 prisoner's names have been engraved.

Haunted Castles

At Bramber Castle, Sussex the children of William de Breose were captured by King John and starved to death. More than 800 years later their pitiful ghosts haunt the grounds, begging for food.

King Charles I was beheaded in 1649, and his headless body taken to Windsor Castle. His ghost now walks the castle grounds, but with his head firmly in place.

Corfe Castle, Dorset was King John's favourite prison. He once starved 22 knights to death there because he thought they were disloyal. Corfe's dungeon tower had a dark and airless basement that could only be reached through a trap door in the floor above. This kind of prison was called an oubliette.

Fyvie Castle, Grampian is one of the most mysterious in the country. No-one will talk of what went on there, but dreadful curses, a ghost and bloodstains that won't go away have led to part of the castle being closed.

In Featherstone Castle, Northumberland, Sir Reginald Fitz Urse was locked up and starved to death. His groans and the clanking of his armour can still be heard.

Prisoner's Memory Game

Prisoner 1: When I was in the dungeon,
I had no food.
Prisoner 2: When I was in the dungeon,
I had no food, and no water
for two days.
Prisoner 3: When I was in the dungeon,
I had no food, no water for
two days, and I was manacled
to the wall.

Take turns, with each prisoner adding something more gruesome. The first prisoner to forget something or make a mistake is beheaded.

Keys

For three players – two prisoners and a gaoler. You need a bunch of keys.

The two prisoners are blindfolded. Only one of them has the chance to escape. The gaoler rattles the keys and chants:
Treacherous traitors
Your time has come
Find the key or die!

Then he throws the keys onto the floor. The prisoners must listen carefully and try to find the keys. Whoever succeeds escapes, then takes a turn as gaoler.

Places to Visit

- Beaumaris Castle, Anglesey – concentric castle, left unfinished.
- Bodiam Castle, East Sussex – a wide moat.
- Dover Castle, Kent – square keep on three storeys with curtain wall.
- Dunstanburgh Castle, Northumberland – built on a cliff edge.
- Kenilworth Castle, Warwickshire – wall towers and square keep, protected by lake.
- Lindisfarne Castle, Northumberland – on Holy Island, cut off by the sea at high tide.
- Pembroke Castle, Dyfed – triangular inner bailey, four storey round keep.
- Richmond Castle, North Yorkshire – curtain wall with square wall towers.
- Rochester Castle, Kent – four storey square keep with forebuilding.
- Tattershall Castle, Lincolnshire – tall keep with double moat.
- Warwick Castle, Warwickshire – motte and bailey with later curtain wall.
- York Castle, North Yorkshire – two motte and bailey castles on a river.

Answers:

Page 9: Castle Quiz:
1. Windsor Castle, England
2. Caernarfon Castle, Wales
3. Corfe Castle, England
4. Pembroke Castle, Wales
5. Balmoral Castle, Scotland.

Page 9: Hidden Words
1. Gatehouse, 2. Keep, 3. Bailey, 4. Motte,
5. Shield, 6. Drawbridge, 7. Moat,
8. Turret, 9. Portcullis, 10. Solar,
11. Garderobe, 12. Barbican

```
G D C B P H H M D L Q G F M F A M A H N E G O O C L
N O L C M G A O F K P M F M G C G H K B I M D M B L
F M Q I M Q Q A N B N C M N J I E M P H B O T H M N
A K A Q S H E T H H K D H M N F O B E D O M U F H O
L E Q F E H G A T E H O U S E N E J I D D G R Q J L
P N A N H K K H N J Q D J B B A G H L L Q B R L J C
N P I D I P Q M K G C N E P H H H I E B G M E D M G
Q Q Q N H P A I N E F Q N K A G P I B Q N O T J B C
C D O N N Q B Q M N J E P L K Q P P F B L B P N O K
B D G S O C Q M F K K K E E P L O I G L H Q B J H N
F C H O C K P F B B E C P G H K R L A O L M E E A F
M C Q L E E N L G H N C H D F B T P M M E Q P L B O
M M Q A B L C J I K I M L E A A C O K D G E Q P Q O
B D L R E O C B B B A I L E Y K U Q H F A K L F Q K
Q D A B Q A B Q M B D H B G H A L G N O R H Q C H K
A K B M B E O P D M P G H H A B L E G N D G C O D L
F I A D G H I D B C L P H F D N I Q N K E P F M Q H
C N R M N L J G D L N M O T T E S P O F R L N Q E E
Q J B K H D O I P E I N N O I G H H F N O I G E B A
F Q I P Q I C C E Q S H I E L D P B E E B N B H F E
F G C Q K D C E B O O S H G K N O Q P I E H D J L P
D O A D K P P J N O J Q Q E D C M L O I H K E O L F
J Q N H M B N E A P J M A Q F Q B P O J K C G E E E
D E O L A G L L M H I A D R A W B R I D G E M K K G
H K I O L G E K Q M E E D L M K N G K I F H H C A F
```

Kingfisher Books, Grisewood & Dempsey Ltd,
Elsley House, 24–30 Great Titchfield Street,
London WIP 7AD.

First published in 1988 by Kingfisher Books
in association with The National Trust.
Reprinted 1988, 1989 (twice), 1990
Text Copyright © Manor Lodge Productions Ltd 1988
Illustrations Copyright © Grisewood & Dempsey Ltd
1988

BRITISH LIBRARY CATALOGUING IN PUBLICATION DATA
Osband, Gillian
  Castles.
  1. Castles – For children
  I. Title   II. Simonds, David   III. Series
  909
ISBN 0 86272 366 3

Edited by Jacqui Bailey and Meg Sanders
Designed by Ben White
Cover design by David Jefferis
Phototypeset by Southern Positives and
Negatives (SPAN), Lingfield, Surrey
Printed in Spain